What Won
about this Book

"We have heard it before, 'you get a car, you get a car, and you get a car.' However, Regina Robinson inspires us to echo, I have a key, you have a key, we all have the keys to unlocking our inner confidence to success. Through trial and error, Ms. Robinson has been battle-tested and has discovered the keys to becoming a winner at self-acceptance, self-belief, and self-love. Her Book is a time-tested and valuable resource that we can use."

—Nellie Jackson, Educator

"This engaging eBook just kept giving and giving! After reading it, I found there was no excuse to not walk confidently in my groove. The confidence assessment was on point! Thanks Regina, my inner confidence groove has been intensified!"

—Maricia Sherman Founder,
HerGroove #thegrooveneverstops

"*Strutting In Your Confidence* is a woman's guide to reassurance. Whether you are in need of a reminder or already have your "strut", this book is for you! Each chapter is filled with wisdom that will help eradicate doubt and build you up through Regina's testimonials of faith, courage and love. The bonus assessment and checklist are both designed to help you shift into a place of confidence and awareness! You have everything to gain by investing in yourself with this read!"

—Kashonna Holland CEO, Simply Kashonna

Fearlessly Strutting In Your Confidence

12 Keys To Unlocking Your Inner-Confidence

Regina Robinson

Published by Regina Robinson
www.reginarobinsonspeaks.com
info@reginarobinsonspeaks.com

Cover design by P2P Branded
www.p2pbranded.com

Book formatted by Katie Brady Design
www.katiebradydesign.com

Printed and bound in the United States of America.

Acknowledgement

It is an honor when one can see the inside of a person's character shine on the outside. I silently lead by example as I allow the manifestation of my work to express my vision, beliefs, philosophies and principles. The footprints I have etched as I journeyed through life have made a tremendous impact on the lives of others as a woman, mother, daughter, sister, aunt, teacher, friend, and professional.

This journal book may have only one official author, however, great work is always accomplished by the multitudes. I would like to take this opportunity to thank my daughter Ashlee Robinson for her love, encouragement, and support, my sister Tarneisha Robinson, mother Brenda Robinson, father Willie Robinson, my nephew Robert Millhouse, and my two brothers for their support, love, patience, and encouragement. It's awesome when you have a supportive family who believes in your vision, supports your dreams, and continues to encourage you daily. To my Coach, Cheryl Wood thank you for pushing me beyond my comfort zone so that others may be blessed. Thanks to my editors and friends Michelle Stover and Nellie Jackson for their countless reviews and support. To my branding team P2P Branded thank you for designing such a flawless book cover. Most importantly, thank you God for walking side by side with me on those days when I felt like giving up. You would quietly whisper a reminder, "Your story does not belong to you." I thank you for purchasing this book and I hope that you will be blessed as you prepare for the next level of your journey.

This Journal Is Dedicated to Women Who Are Ready To Fearlessly Strut In Their Confidence With Power, Poise, & Purpose

As women we often show up; yet, we doubt our ability to represent ourselves due to a lack of confidence in our value. However, in order for us to operate in our immense power, we must be willing to break the limitations of fear, doubt, and negative beliefs. The beautiful words of the late Maya Angelou reminds us that; "You may encounter many defeats, but you must not be defeated. In fact, it may be necessary to encounter the defeats, so you can know how you are, what you can rise from, and how you can still come out of it." Queen Latifah said it best when she declared: "Ladies First, Ladies First"; Chaka Khan shared it with grace and confidence when she uttered the words; "I'm Every Woman! It's All In Me!" Let's not forget Beyoncé's Anthem: "Who Run The World? Girls!"

Ladies it's our time to take ownership as we:

#ShowUpInPower,

#BeTheAuthenticYou,

#WalkInYourGreatness

#FearlesslyStruttingInYourConfidence

Foreword

*F*earlessly *Strutting In Your Confidence – 12-Keys to Unlocking Your Inner Confidence* written by Inner Confidence Strategist Regina Robinson is an empowering and thought-provoking written work of art that challenges its readers to show up in their power, remain authentic, and take ownership of their lives by means of increased internal confidence. This book will resonate deeply with all who are ready to remove limitations in order to start building confidence in their dreams and possibilities.

*F*earlessly *Strutting In Your Confidence* provides 12 powerful keys to greater confidence and life fulfillment through self-work, self-assessment, and a commitment to becoming a better version of who you already are. If you are done playing small, this book is just what you need to create a drastic shift in the direction of living a bigger, bolder life. The transformational content contained within sparks a flame that energizes you to fall in love with who you are at your core and to value yourself in spite of your faults, failures, and disappointments. Through a host of checklists, assessments, reflections, and decrees you will find yourself on a fast track to increased confidence and creating the reality you want. As you turn each page, you will be reminded of the need to shift your daily internal conversation, rise above your fears, and abandon the shackles that negatively bind you to your past.

Each powerful key contained in this book will equip you to consistently nurture your possibilities without letup. You will rediscover a deep soul commitment to getting laser focused on your destiny instead of remaining complacent in a life of mediocrity. Fearlessly Strutting In Your Confidence will stretch you to take bigger risks in your life and to develop behaviors and patterns that support your overall growth. If you are a person who is committed to living with intention and fulfilling your purpose, this book is the answer you've been searching for!

As a Global Women's Empowerment Speaker & Coach with a mission to empower and equip women to walk in their greatness without apologies or regrets, Fearlessly Strutting In Your Confidence is perfectly aligned with this mission. It is indeed a powerful reflection and extension of the importance of pushing beyond your comforts and mastering the confidence to pursue your most unrealistic dreams. Fearlessly Strutting In Your Confidence will equip you to do what it takes to claim power over your present and your future.

As you allow the powerful thoughts in this book to penetrate in your spirit, remember that nothing has the power to hold you back from confidently pursuing greatness in your life except you. Be sure to keep a copy of Fearlessly Strutting In Your Confidence nearby as a valuable and relevant resource that will prompt you to take actions consistent with your desires. Remember, NOW is your time to confidently build the life you want – Playtime Is Over!

—Cheryl Wood
International Speaker & Transformational Speaking Coach
www.CherylWoodEmpowers.com

How I Discovered My Keys To Win

I am passionate about helping women unlock their inner-confidence because I know what it feels like to lack confidence, have doubts about being good enough, question your worth, and fear success. I'm clear about what it feels like to be afraid to acknowledge your own ability to win.

As I continue on my journey, I am aware of the importance of lifting up my sisters. I stand firm today because of the sacrifices of the many women whose shoulders I have stood upon. Today, I declare and decree with you as I shine the spotlight on you my sister as you confidently propel into your next level Fearlessly Strutting with Power, Poise & Purpose! However, I am a testament that it is possible to unlock your inner-confidence and show up in your power. Wherever you are today, put a praise on all God has in store for you.

Table of Contents

Introduction

I am humbly grateful that you have decided to go on this journey with me to unlock your inner-confidence and unapologetically pursue your next level of greatness. This journal is truly an expression from my heart. Every key is a representation of the many scars and bruises I have encountered along my journey to discovering how to walk in my greatness. The confidence that I have today comes from my JOY in the Lord. I once questioned, "God are You sure You want to use ME?" He answered, "yes, with the very scars and bruises I have allowed you to encounter so that others can see that as long as they trust in Me all things will work together for their good.

Today, I am super excited to unveil the twelve keys to help you understand the importance of valuing your worth, acknowledging your unique gifts, and unlocking your inner-confidence to unapologetically walk into your greatness. I will help you discover your keys, and at the end of each key, there will be an opportunity for you to reflect, journal, and declare and decree about the actions you will take as you catapult into your next level.

Let's first start by defining **Inner-Confidence.** Inner-Confidence comes from the Latin origin: from the verb *confidere*, meaning, ***"to have full trust in oneself"*** spiritually, mentally, emotionally, and physically.

Key 1

Unveil Your Love Today

Self-Love

Self-Love – regard for one's own well-being and happiness.

$\mathcal{O}$ften we assume that we love ourselves without really examining and asking ourselves the very question "Do you love me or do you just tolerate me?" Yes, take a minute to wrap your mind around that question. Wow! I'm sure that hit home for someone. I am sure most of you answered: I love myself, but if we dig deeper are we really in love with ourselves? Some might question what's the difference? Well there is a true differentiation. I know everyone reading this has been in relationships where you loved a woman or man; however, you stopped being in love with them. Essentially, you stopped valuing them, lost interest, stopped paying them attention like you did in the beginning, and distanced yourself from them. **The truth is some of you are treating yourself the same way!**

I'm sure you are saying, "Ok then, how can I begin to fall in LOVE with myself all over again?" I encourage you to:

- Stop comparing yourself to others. Focus on being the best version of you. Remember you are unique in your own way.

- Learn to receive love, compliments, and most important-ly help from others. Show yourself love by declaring, "I Love Me." This sounds cliché, but can I tell you it works. When you can declare to yourself the words, "I Love Me" that is when you recognize the value you possess.

- Treat yourself! Often times we give so much of ourselves to others that we forget to give to ourselves. Today, spoil yourself by going out to your favorite restaurant, buy yourself a gift just because, or just go to a place you love.

In order to tap into your confidence, loving yourself from the inside out is KEY.

Reflection Question

Write down five things you love about yourself and share why you love them?

_____

_____

_____

_____

_____

_____

_____

_____

_____

_____

_____

_____

IT'S YOUR TIME TO SHINE TODAY
FEARLESSY STRUT IN YOUR CONFIDENCE WITH
POWER, POISE, & PURPOSE!!

Reflection Question

If you had to write yourself a love letter, what would it say?
Take this time to write a letter reuniting your love for you…

_____

_____

_____

_____

_____

_____

_____

_____

_____

_____

_____

_____

_____

IT'S YOUR TIME TO SHINE TODAY
FEARLESSY STRUT IN YOUR CONFIDENCE WITH
POWER, POISE, & PURPOSE!!

Reflect, Prepare, and Take Action

_____

_____

_____

_____

_____

_____

_____

_____

_____

_____

_____

_____

_____

_____

_____

_____

_____

_____

_____

Reflect, Prepare, and Take Action

_____

_____

_____

_____

_____

_____

_____

_____

_____

_____

_____

_____

_____

_____

_____

_____

_____

_____

Reflect, Prepare, and Take Action

_____

_____

_____

_____

_____

_____

_____

_____

_____

_____

_____

_____

_____

_____

_____

_____

Key 2

Drown Out The Noise

Internal Dialogue

Internal Dialogue – reaction to what we say to ourselves about what happens in our lives.

"We all talk to ourselves. Our internal dialogue either tells us that we can conquer our fears and accomplish our goals or we allow our internal dialogue to create unnecessary obstacles that defeat us."

Let me first start by acknowledging, I talk to myself all the time. I believed that as long as I didn't answer back, I was not crazy. However, the problem was that my conversations were always negative. We often have a problem when others speak negatively about us, when in fact we need to take ownership of the negative comments, feedback, and conversations we have with ourselves. The negative conversations I was having with myself became the norm — a continuous cycle of self-doubt, fear, and disbelief. There were countless times I talked myself out of great opportunities, because I allowed my negative thoughts, "I can't, I'm not good enough, What if" to cloud out the positive ones, "I can, You are awesome, and When you."

Gain control over your negative thoughts as you:

- Drown out the noise / negative dialogue and listen for God's voice as you encourage and empower yourself.

- Acknowledge the negative sabotage that is raging war within your mind and reclaim the power of positive thoughts.

- Refuse to entertain any thoughts or conservations that don't empower you to move forward in greatness.

I challenge you to release the negative chatter and begin speaking positively into your life in anticipation of all God has in store for you as you move forward in your journey.

Reflection Question

What negative emotions have you allowed to stop you from pursuing your greatness in life?

_____

_____

_____

_____

_____

_____

_____

_____

_____

_____

_____

_____

_____

IT'S YOUR TIME TO SHINE TODAY
FEARLESSY STRUT IN YOUR CONFIDENCE WITH
POWER, POISE, & PURPOSE!!

Reflection Question

Write a letter to yourself today declaring you will no longer allow the negativity of your voice or others' opinions to rent or occupy space in your mind.

_____

_____

_____

_____

_____

_____

_____

_____

_____

_____

_____

_____

IT'S YOUR TIME TO SHINE TODAY
FEARLESSY STRUT IN YOUR CONFIDENCE WITH
POWER, POISE, & PURPOSE!!

Reflect, Prepare, and Take Action

_____

_____

_____

_____

_____

_____

_____

_____

_____

_____

_____

_____

_____

_____

_____

_____

_____

_____

Reflect, Prepare, and Take Action

Reflect, Prepare, and Take Action

_____

_____

_____

_____

_____

_____

_____

_____

_____

_____

_____

_____

_____

_____

_____

_____

_____

Key 3

You Are Worthy
of Greatness

Self-Worth

Self-Worth – the sense of one's own value or worth as a person; self-esteem; self-respect.

If you had to rate your worth, what would you score yourself on a scale of 1–10 with 10 being you are awesome and worthy of all God has in store for you? Did you automatically score yourself as a 10 or did you hesitate and go into deep thought? If someone had asked me this question a few years back, I would have hesitated and not given myself a 10. Why? For a long time I doubted my self-worth because I lacked confidence in me. I had the outer layer of confidence but my inner-confidence was shattered. I had become immune to the wounds on the inside by masking them with outer concealment.

As women, it is key that we begin to search within and value ourselves as we are despite our past faults, failures, and disappointments. All of these areas are just temporary scars that heal. So today grant yourself permission to heal. I often believed that I was scared and broken and often asked God, how can You use me to help others? His response: I can use even YOU! I know that in life we will fall, fail, and have questionable days, but I can assure you that if you allow God to step in, He will teach you valuable lessons in the midst of your unknowns.

In order to move forward, you have to be willing to "face forward" so I encourage you to:

- Acknowledge that your passion and purpose is for you to share your story with others. I am sharing this message with you today because I understand that my story matters.

- Accept yourself just as you are and as you grow into the person God has destined for you to be.

- Abandon the shackles that are holding and binding you to your past. Know that God is willing to use "EVEN YOU."

From this day forward, stop questioning whether you deserve the greatness God has in store for you and begin walking in your Greatness! It is time for you to release who you believe you are suppose to be and instead give yourself permission to allow God to show you exactly who you are destined to be.

Reflection Question

In order for others to value your worth, you must first determine your own value. What value have you placed on your self-worth?

_____

_____

_____

_____

_____

_____

_____

_____

_____

_____

_____

_____

IT'S YOUR TIME TO SHINE TODAY
FEARLESSY STRUT IN YOUR CONFIDENCE WITH
POWER, POISE, & PURPOSE!!

Reflection Question

What are some areas that you must begin to allow yourself to heal in order to accept yourself as the awesome woman God has destined you to be?

_____

_____

_____

_____

_____

_____

_____

_____

_____

_____

_____

_____

_____

IT'S YOUR TIME TO SHINE TODAY
FEARLESSY STRUT IN YOUR CONFIDENCE WITH
POWER, POISE, & PURPOSE!!

Reflect, Prepare, and Take Action

Reflect, Prepare, and Take Action

_____

_____

_____

_____

_____

_____

_____

_____

_____

_____

_____

_____

_____

_____

Reflect, Prepare, and Take Action

_____

_____

_____

_____

_____

_____

_____

_____

_____

_____

_____

_____

_____

_____

_____

_____

_____

_____

Key 4

Release All Limiting
Beliefs

Self-Belief

Self-Belief – confidence in oneself and one's ability.

Trusting the wisdom you have will guide you towards your purpose. You have to begin declaring that you are a winner even before you win. Don't count yourself out before even trying.

I'm sure you're asking, "How can I begin to move forward?" I encourage you to:

- *Eliminate doubt...*stop counting yourself out before you even get in the game. See yourself as a winner before you win, declare that all your programs are full don't wait, celebrate now.

- *Expose fear...*don't allow fear to cripple you. What do you have to lose? Most of us never reach success because we throw in the towel too early (often right before the blessing). The saying is, "if your dreams don't scare you they are not big enough."

- *Encourage yourself...*by releasing the negative conversations you are having with yourself: I can't...What if? ...I don't think that's possible. I declare today that you will begin to change your conversation and instead speak life: When I...I know if I...All things are possible.

Push beyond your self-limiting boundaries and say YES to opportunities that will allow you to stretch as you learn, grow, and fail. When you release comfort, there lies your greatness!

Repeat after me:

I believe in my dreams even if no one else does.
I believe that everyday something great is going to happen.
I believe that endless possibilities are in store for me.
I declare that all things are possible.
I am ready to receive all God has in store for me.

Reflection Question

Declare victory over your limiting beliefs today by declaring I will no longer allow negative beliefs to paralyze me from success. What limiting beliefs are you holding on to?

_____

_____

_____

_____

_____

_____

_____

_____

_____

_____

_____

_____

_____

IT'S YOUR TIME TO SHINE TODAY
FEARLESSY STRUT IN YOUR CONFIDENCE WITH
POWER, POISE, & PURPOSE!!

Reflection Question

If you believe this is the year to walk in your greatness, what does that look like (mind, body, and spirit)?

_____

_____

_____

_____

_____

_____

_____

_____

_____

_____

_____

_____

_____

IT'S YOUR TIME TO SHINE TODAY
FEARLESSY STRUT IN YOUR CONFIDENCE WITH
POWER, POISE, & PURPOSE!!

Reflect, Prepare, and Take Action

Reflect, Prepare, and Take Action

Reflect, Prepare, and Take Action

_____

_____

_____

_____

_____

_____

_____

_____

_____

_____

_____

_____

_____

_____

_____

_____

Key 5

Rise Above Your Fears

Fear

Fear – to be afraid; worried about something or someone.

When you rise above FEAR, your
destiny will be waiting.

Oftentimes we go through life attaching ourselves to the crippling effect of worry, fright, and apprehension. We often hold ourselves hostage to the bondages of: Fear of failure, Fear of rejection, Fear of judgment, Fear of inadequacy, and Fear of success. It's not until we openly reveal our biggest secrets to the world, that we can truly overcome the FEAR that keeps us paralyzed from triumphing towards our dreams. What big secrets have you allowed FEAR to keep you from achieving?

For so long I allowed fear to keep me from pursuing all the big dreams God birthed within me. It wasn't until one day I decided to take control of my FEAR and reveal my secrets to the world. In fact, that is why you're reading this journal book today. Now don't get me wrong, I was fearful up until the last word you will read on the very last page of this journal. However, I recognize that fear is never going to go away. We control the credit that we allow fear to take in our lives.

I set off to write this book celebrating me for the first time. I stopped looking back and began gazing forward to what tomorrow may bring and understanding that God wanted me to share this book with YOU. As you read the words from this page, I am celebrating with you in advance as you begin

Fearlessly Strutting In Your Confidence with Power, Poise, & Purpose! From this day forward I encourage you to:

- Do it even if you end up getting it wrong; you can learn from the lessons you encountered along the way

- Accept the things you can control and lay aside what is out of your control

- With every passing day celebrate without fear, hesitation, or doubt and accept that you cannot predict the future

Isn't it beautiful to be able to move forward even when fear arises? Remember that tomorrow will always bring new opportunities so don't allow fear to keep you detained in today and overlook the possibilities of tomorrow. I encourage you to begin smiling, embracing, and celebrating all that God has birthed within you as you dream big.

Reflection Question

What are some areas where fear has crippled you?

_____

_____

_____

_____

_____

_____

_____

_____

_____

_____

_____

_____

_____

_____

IT'S YOUR TIME TO SHINE TODAY
FEARLESSY STRUT IN YOUR CONFIDENCE WITH
POWER, POISE, & PURPOSE!!

Reflection Question

Write fear a personal letter taking back ownership of your thoughts, energy, and future destiny.

_____

_____

_____

_____

_____

_____

_____

_____

_____

_____

_____

_____

IT'S YOUR TIME TO SHINE TODAY
FEARLESSY STRUT IN YOUR CONFIDENCE WITH
POWER, POISE, & PURPOSE!!

Reflect, Prepare, and Take Action

Reflect, Prepare, and Take Action

_____

_____

_____

_____

_____

_____

_____

_____

_____

_____

_____

_____

_____

_____

_____

_____

Reflect, Prepare, and Take Action

_____

_____

_____

_____

_____

_____

_____

_____

_____

_____

_____

_____

_____

_____

_____

_____

_____

_____

Key 6

Your Behaviors Become Your Habits

Behavior

Behavior – the way in which one acts or conducts oneself.

Keep your thoughts positive because your thoughts become your words; Keep your words positive because your words become your behavior; Keep your behavior positive because your behavior becomes your habits.

–AUTHOR UNKNOWN

When you wake up every day, open your eyes and embrace a new day. Begin your day with the power of new possibilities, dreams, and expectations. Are you open to the surprise of a new day that God has set before you? If so, don't allow the worries of tomorrow and life to remove you from staying in touch with the essence of you. Remember there will always be only one you in this world so why not live your life to the fullest. Remember life is a journey filled with surprises. Pause along the way as you:

- Take a moment to acknowledge who you are

- Embrace the brand new expectations of what God has in store for you

- Take life's ride not expecting the answers to every stop along the way to your destination

Now is your time. What path will you follow? Remember it's ok to be different, because God did not design you to be like others. Along the way there will be mistakes, but now is the time to take chances without regret. You don't want to look back and wonder about all the surprises life had in store that you missed out on because you were afraid of embracing a new day. Everyday day as you gaze in the mirror grateful for the faith and confidence God has bestowed upon you, remind yourself that:

- You are an awesome and amazing woman

- You are a woman filled with strength and power

- You are a woman who is fearless and destined for greatness

- You are a woman who continues to win in life

- You are a woman who boldly walks in her confidence

Every day open up your heart and allow the diamond that you are to shine so bright that when you show up, the world will see your fearlessness of power, poise, and purpose.

Reflection Question

In what ways are you allowing the WORDS you speak to yourself to dictate your behavior?

_____

_____

_____

_____

_____

_____

_____

_____

_____

_____

_____

_____

IT'S YOUR TIME TO SHINE TODAY
FEARLESSY STRUT IN YOUR CONFIDENCE WITH
POWER, POISE, & PURPOSE!!

Reflection Question

What regrets of behavior have you allowed to possess power over your today?

_____

_____

_____

_____

_____

_____

_____

_____

_____

_____

_____

_____

IT'S YOUR TIME TO SHINE TODAY
FEARLESSY STRUT IN YOUR CONFIDENCE WITH
POWER, POISE, & PURPOSE!!

Reflect, Prepare, and Take Action

Reflect, Prepare, and Take Action

_____

_____

_____

_____

_____

_____

_____

_____

_____

_____

_____

_____

_____

_____

_____

_____

Reflect, Prepare, and Take Action

_____

_____

_____

_____

_____

_____

_____

_____

_____

_____

_____

_____

_____

_____

_____

_____

_____

_____

_____

Key 7

Don't Risk Never Trying

Risk

Risk – an unforeseen possibility that you will experience a loss.

If you win you will be happy; if you lose you will be wise.
—Author Unknown

Don't make fear powerful by placing layers around the dreams God has given you because of the Fear of Failure. In order to fulfill your dreams, passion, and purpose you must be willing to…TAKE RISKS? "Shish"…do you hear that? It's time for you to start listening to the voice that softly reminds you that it's time to break down the walls of fear, doubt, and worry. What are you waiting for? Better yet, who are you waiting for?

Don't become satisfied with a mediocre life when you can DREAM BIG. Unless you stretch yourself beyond your comfort zone and take risks, you will never reach your full potential. Stop waiting on your dreams to happen tomorrow, instead make your move today and define your destiny. Success is not going to come to you; in fact, you have to go after the success you desire. Along the way, you will encounter disappointments, bruises, and failures. However, they are just stepping-stones in your journey. When you weather the storm and remember your WHY, there lies your destiny.

Remember it's not about how hard you get hit; instead, it's about your willingness to keep pressing forward in the midst of the blows. Don't allow the fear of taking risks to be more powerful than your reward of freely living out your dreams, passions, and purpose. Most people often fear the darkness that comes from taking risks, but will overlook the light that will begin to illuminate as they become one step closer to their success.

Are you ready to boldly move forward today without limitations and begin writing a brand new chapter in your story? If you answered yes, now is the time to walk in your power and play all out. Every day wake up with the expectation that today is your day to WIN.

Our deepest fear is not that we are inadequate. Our deepest fear is that we are powerful beyond measure. It is our light, not our darkness that most frightens us.

—Marianne Williamson

Reflection Question

What would it take for you to step out of your comfort zone and take bigger risks in life?

_____

_____

_____

_____

_____

_____

_____

_____

_____

_____

_____

IT'S YOUR TIME TO SHINE TODAY
FEARLESSY STRUT IN YOUR CONFIDENCE WITH
POWER, POISE, & PURPOSE!!

Reflection Question

Are you willing to take bigger risks if it means greater results?

_____

_____

_____

_____

_____

_____

_____

_____

_____

_____

_____

_____

IT'S YOUR TIME TO SHINE TODAY
FEARLESSY STRUT IN YOUR CONFIDENCE WITH
POWER, POISE, & PURPOSE!!

Reflect, Prepare, and Take Action

_____

_____

_____

_____

_____

_____

_____

_____

_____

_____

_____

_____

_____

_____

_____

_____

_____

Reflect, Prepare, and Take Action

Reflect, Prepare, and Take Action

Key 8

The Value of Your Circle

Accountability

Accountability – the quality or state of being accountable to accept responsibility for one's actions.

As iron sharpens iron, so one man sharpens another.

—PROVERBS 27:17 NIV

A stadium is filled with many seats; however, only those willing to make the investment can sit on the front row. Jim Rohn said it best, "You are the average of the 5 people you spend the most time with." Remember, Jesus had 12 disciples, but only a chosen few were considered his right hand man. So if Jesus felt so strongly about which disciples He chose as His closest inner circle, why wouldn't you value yours the same? Who's occupying space on your front row? As you evaluate your inner circle ask yourself the following questions:

- Do I admire their qualities?

- Do I desire to be like them?

- Do they add value to my life?

- Can I trust them whole-heartedly with my life?

- Can I learn from them?

Take a minute and reflect. Are the people on your front row propelling you forward spiritually, mentally, physically, and emotionally? If not, it's time to evaluate the people you have granted VIP access into your life.

Most of us have people riding along for the journey, but instead of encouraging you, they drain you. Instead of empowering you, they wallow with you. Despite your willingness to rise, they continue pulling you down. It's clear that if you're the only one encouraging and empowering your circle of influence, it's time for an upgrade.

> If you're not wiling to let go of the wrong people, how do you expect to have room for the right people?

Surround yourself with people who inspire, celebrate, and push you forward, while always keeping your best interest at heart. You know the people in your inner circle are one hundred percent committed because they:

- Pray with you, encourage you, and remind you of how awesome you are

- Expose the realities of life while holding you accountable in a loving way

- Are honest with you even when you're not being honest with yourself

- Are there to give you godly wisdom, listen to your ideas, problems, and offer you sound advice

- Are willing to share their greatness with you from a place of experience

> Create an inner circle that not only understands your journey, but will join with you in Faith as you walk in your destiny.

Reflection Question

What does having communities of like-minded people mean to your growth spiritually, mentally, emotionally, and physically?

_____

_____

_____

_____

_____

_____

_____

_____

_____

_____

_____

_____

IT'S YOUR TIME TO SHINE TODAY
FEARLESSY STRUT IN YOUR CONFIDENCE WITH
POWER, POISE, & PURPOSE!!

Reflection Question

How can an accountability partner support you in becoming the best version of YOU?

_____

_____

_____

_____

_____

_____

_____

_____

_____

_____

_____

IT'S YOUR TIME TO SHINE TODAY
FEARLESSY STRUT IN YOUR CONFIDENCE WITH
POWER, POISE, & PURPOSE!!

Reflect, Prepare, and Take Action

Reflect, Prepare, and Take Action

_____

_____

_____

_____

_____

_____

_____

_____

_____

_____

_____

_____

_____

_____

_____

_____

Reflect, Prepare, and Take Action

_____

_____

_____

_____

_____

_____

_____

_____

_____

_____

_____

_____

_____

_____

_____

_____

Key 9

Powerful Beyond Measure

Power

Power – the capacity or ability to direct or influence the behavior of others.

Women are often stereotyped as emotional; however, I believe we are just passionate explorers in pursuit of excellence who are willing to do what others can't imagine. We believe in getting the job done, avoiding procrastination, and doing what it takes to accomplish a goal.

Where we often fall short as women is acknowledging that we don't have all the answers. In order to envision the power of the words, wisdom, and gifts God has given us, we must be willing to gain the knowledge necessary to operate in our power. Are you prepared to use your power to leverage and maximize your potential as God elevates you into your next dimension? The problem that arises is that as women we often doubt our Power before we get to our next level. Our true power is ignited when we make the decision to enhance who we are despite our fears, doubts, and failures. Now is your time to show up in your power but in order to reach the peak you must be willing to persevere as you:

- *Fail Early*…We all fail early on; however, it's what you take from the failure that matters most. So stop putting the pressure of being perfect on you.

- *Fail Often*…Don't get caught up in the details of how often you fail; instead, look at the bigger picture and learn from the lessons as you propel forward.

- *Fail Forward*…As you move forward, always be willing to adapt and evolve as you learn, grow, and lead.

Today as you begin to walk in your power, you must be prepared to weather the storm. I challenge you to walk in the Power of who you are today, in preparation for walking in the power of who you will become. Successfully walking in your Power will require your willingness to remind yourself daily:

- *I am powerful beyond measure…because God has destined me for greatness*

- *I am powerful beyond measure…as I stretch beyond my comfort zone in order to fulfill my dreams*

- *I am powerful beyond measure…because I value the power God has given me to rise above mediocrity*

- *I am powerful beyond measure…because I am a winner*

- *I am powerful beyond measure…because I understand that nothing in life is easy, but when you give it your all the reward far outweighs the difficulties*

- *I am powerful beyond measure…because I know it is possible to do all things*

- *I am powerful beyond measure…because I understand that God gave my vision to me and everyone does not have to understand it*

- *I am powerful beyond measure…because I don't allow the fears of others to stop me from believing all things are possible*

- *I am powerful beyond measure…because although fear and doubt knock at my door, I keep moving forward to my destiny*

- *I am powerful beyond measure…because every trial and tribulation I have encountered has prepared me for who I am today*

- *I am powerful beyond measure…because I understand that my WHY is greater than any obstacles I will face in life*

- *I am powerful beyond measure…because saying "no" to my dreams and passions is not an option*

Reflection Question

What does the word power mean to you?

_____

_____

_____

_____

_____

_____

_____

_____

_____

_____

_____

_____

IT'S YOUR TIME TO SHINE TODAY
FEARLESSY STRUT IN YOUR CONFIDENCE WITH
POWER, POISE, & PURPOSE!!

Reflection Question

Are you boldly showing up in your power or are you hiding in the background?

_____

_____

_____

_____

_____

_____

_____

_____

_____

_____

_____

_____

IT'S YOUR TIME TO SHINE TODAY
FEARLESSY STRUT IN YOUR CONFIDENCE WITH
POWER, POISE, & PURPOSE!!

Reflect, Prepare, and Take Action

_____

_____

_____

_____

_____

_____

_____

_____

_____

_____

_____

_____

_____

_____

_____

_____

_____

_____

Reflect, Prepare, and Take Action

Reflect, Prepare, and Take Action

Reflect, Prepare, and Take Action

Key 10

Unlock Your
Inner-Confidence

Confidence

Confidence – a feeling of self-assurance arising from one's appreciation of one's own abilities or qualities.

Yes, yes you look good, you are amazing, you are fearless; you are so confident! You know you are faking, so why are you pretending? You are not that confident. I hope no one is looking, because if they look close enough they will see I am not confident. If only they knew I wear a mask to cover my scars, imperfections, and bruises.

How many of you have ever pretended to be (or know someone who pretends to be) someone other than who they really are? If we can be honest with ourselves at some point, we have all pretended to be someone we are not. I know all too well what it feels like to go through the motions pretending everything was great because I was afraid to admit I was broken. Instead, I would reply with a smile, "I'm blessed and highly favored." When inside, the pain and insecurity of what I believed to be my inadequacies come through. Am I enough? Am I worthy? Will people value me? All of these questions became my daily dose of inspiration.

No matter how much I tried to convince everyone else that I was confident and had it all together, every time I looked in the mirror I was reminded of my imperfections, disappointments, and what I believed to be my life failures. It wasn't until I had the tough conversation of asking myself, "Who are you really? Do you like who you see?" As I began to reflect, I realized the person I was presenting did not mirror my truth. In fact, I almost fooled myself.

I quickly realized my life echoed the very words of the great Les Brown: "If you don't program your life, your life will program you." I decided to no longer allow my past to predict my future and instead allowed the power within me, to fuel my belief that I could accomplish all God destined for me as long as I was willing to:

- *Step outside my comfort zone and take responsibility* – I didn't need all the answers to try. However, in order to get to my destination, I had to be willing to first start. Today take your first STEP.

- *Unapologetically Walk in my Greatness* – I take responsibility that I can't control how others perceive me, but walking in my power was something I had complete control of as long as I was willing to believe in myself and have faith that I could accomplish all things. Today, walk in your GREATNESS.

- *Acknowledge my fears* – I take responsibility that I have control of the amount of credit I give to fear by acknowledging that when it arises, I have the power to catapult it immediately by encouraging and empowering myself to believe I have everything within me. Today, believe in YOU.

- *Value my worth* – I take responsibility that in order to understand my value, I must first acknowledge how I see myself, what I believe about myself, and release the limitations I place on myself as I pursue my dreams, own my uniqueness, and accept all God has in store for me as I walk in my purpose. Today, value your WORTH.

- *Remind myself that I am awesome* – I take responsibility that it has never been about winning the race, but the tenacity and endurance I maintained along the journey while willingly running the course, understanding it is not over until I win. Today, declare you are a winner, even before you WIN.

When working at your dreams; the harder the battle, the sweeter the victory. When it's hard and there is a struggle, what you become in the process is far more important than the dream. The person you become, the character you build, the courage you develop and the faith that you manifest, allows you to look in the mirror and see a different kind of person with a different spirit. People can see your change.

—LES BROWN

Reflection Question

On a scale of 1-10, with 10 being the highest, what is your confidence level?

_____

_____

_____

_____

_____

_____

_____

_____

_____

_____

_____

IT'S YOUR TIME TO SHINE TODAY
FEARLESSY STRUT IN YOUR CONFIDENCE WITH
POWER, POISE, & PURPOSE!!

Reflection Question

Confidence comes not from always being right but from not fearing being wrong.

—AUTHOR UNKNOWN

What does this quote mean to you?

_____

_____

_____

_____

_____

_____

_____

_____

_____

_____

IT'S YOUR TIME TO SHINE TODAY
FEARLESSY STRUT IN YOUR CONFIDENCE WITH
POWER, POISE, & PURPOSE!!

Reflect, Prepare, and Take Action

Reflect, Prepare, and Take Action

Reflect, Prepare, and Take Action

_____

_____

_____

_____

_____

_____

_____

_____

_____

_____

_____

_____

_____

_____

_____

_____

_____

Reflect, Prepare, and Take Action

Key 11

Be the Authentic You

Authenticity

Authenticity – the quality of being authentic; not false or copied; genuine; real.

Authenticity is the daily practice of letting go of who we think we're suppose to be and embracing who we are.

—BRENE BRIAN

Acknowledging who you are is the beginning of discovering the authentic you. Unless you open yourself up, you will never receive the destiny God has in store for you. As long as you are mimicking others your greatness will never be achieved, however, the minute you become transparent and vulnerable, replacement of you is impossible.

Often times we go through life concerned about making others happy in being who they believe we should be. We forget about our own happiness. You have the freedom to be in competition with your own uniqueness and gifts as you fulfill your predestined divine purpose. The problem is we give up the power to our dreams, because we:

- *Watch others dream instead of focusing on our own.* We will never manifest our dreams spending time getting to know others' instead of focusing our time on getting to know ourselves.

- *Live vicariously through the validity of others.* We will never reach our full potential if we allow others' limitations of us to become our limits and beliefs. Stop comparing your success to others' level of accomplishments.

- *Never allow others' conception of what our dreams should be cloud the vision God gave to us.* We will never bring our vision to reality concerning ourselves about what others think; instead we must change the game and start dreaming bigger than we can imagine. Take a chance and determine your rules to success you will always come out a winner.

- *Don't conform to the norm out of Fear.* We will never shine until we are willing to break off the shackles of Fear. "Dare to be You, Dare to be Me. Dare to be different and unique. I'm going to be the best me I can be." – Carmen Calhoun

I challenge you today to begin spending intimate time getting to know, love, and understand yourself, so you can confidently own who you are without the approval of others. Remember, everyone else is already taken, so be the best authentic you. Define your true value today.

Reflection Question

Do you struggle with being the authentic you because of your fear of how others might perceive you?

_____

_____

_____

_____

_____

_____

_____

_____

_____

_____

_____

_____

IT'S YOUR TIME TO SHINE TODAY
FEARLESSY STRUT IN YOUR CONFIDENCE WITH
POWER, POISE, & PURPOSE!!

Reflection Question

Write yourself a letter explaining why it is important for you to show up as the authentic you.

_____

_____

_____

_____

_____

_____

_____

_____

_____

_____

_____

_____

IT'S YOUR TIME TO SHINE TODAY
FEARLESSY STRUT IN YOUR CONFIDENCE WITH
POWER, POISE, & PURPOSE!!

Reflect, Prepare, and Take Action

Reflect, Prepare, and Take Action

Reflect, Prepare, and Take Action

_____

_____

_____

_____

_____

_____

_____

_____

_____

_____

_____

_____

_____

_____

_____

_____

_____

_____

_____

Key 12

Pursue Your Purpose
with Passion

Passion

Passion – Passion is when you put more energy into something than is required. It is more than just enthusiasm or excitement. Passion is ambition that is materialized into action to put as much heart, mind, body and soul into something as is possible.

Behind every success is effort; behind every effort is passion; behind every passion is someone with the courage to try.

—AUTHOR UNKNOWN

*A*re you allowing your fire to dim because you continue to question if today is the day to pursue your purpose? If not today, when? While you're standing on the sidelines questioning and awaiting God, God is waiting on You to show up and take ownership of your purpose. Your resilience to grow to the next level will keep you moving forward when fear, failure, setbacks, and challenges arise. When you can release the fear of the unknown then and only then, will your purpose be revealed.

When you sit in front of a fireplace watching the fire burn and don't add more wood, the flames will eventually disappear. Just like in life, mistakes teach you lessons, disappointments make you wiser, and detours often lead you to your final destination. So remember in order to keep your fire burning, you must refuel your passion just as if it was a log in a fireplace.

The pain in your story will continuously keep the passion for your "Why" burning. With the tenacity of your bright lights glowing, others will be drawn to the authentic you. Growing weary in your passion will stop you from reaching the success of helping others. I believe experiencing struggle along the way to our destination is a sure sign that we are in pursuit of our divine purpose.

Now is the time to connect your passion to your purpose with a sense of urgency by:

- Allowing your passions to create new possibilities

- Knowing your strength comes in understanding there are no limitations

- Releasing doubt and leaping into your purpose

- Discovering your inner-self will lead you to your destiny

You can't expect to reach the next level of your potential doing old things with the expectation of new results. In fact, you must be willing to do what others will not. **"The dream is free. The hustle is sold separately."** Your passion to succeed must burn so intensely that the fire within pushes you to achieve the un-achievable. Awaken your purpose today and illuminate the possibilities as you re-fuel your passion.

When you find your purpose, you won't have to work hard to chase your provision; your provision will chase after you.

—Bishop T.D. Jakes

Reflection Question

What is holding you back from sharing your gifts with the world?

_____

_____

_____

_____

_____

_____

_____

_____

_____

_____

_____

IT'S YOUR TIME TO SHINE TODAY
FEARLESSY STRUT IN YOUR CONFIDENCE WITH
POWER, POISE, & PURPOSE!!

Reflection Question

Are you waiting on things to be perfect before you take action and ignite your passion? If so, take one step towards your purpose today.

_____

_____

_____

_____

_____

_____

_____

_____

_____

_____

IT'S YOUR TIME TO SHINE TODAY
FEARLESSY STRUT IN YOUR CONFIDENCE WITH
POWER, POISE, & PURPOSE!!

Reflect, Prepare, and Take Action

Reflect, Prepare, and Take Action

_____

_____

_____

_____

_____

_____

_____

_____

_____

_____

_____

_____

_____

_____

_____

_____

_____

Reflect, Prepare, and Take Action

Inner-Confidence Assessment

In discovering my keys, I had to first be honest with myself and admit I needed to make changes on what I believed about myself in terms of my own negative self-talk, self-doubt, and fear. I hope the inner-confidence checklist and assessment below will help you discover your confidence level as you prepare to move from *"Fear and Doubt to Certainty and Confidence."*

Don't overthink the questions just record your first response.
(1-Usually / 2-Frequently / 3-Sometimes
/ 4-Occassionally / 5-Rarely)

_____ Before making decisions, I often consult with others.

_____ Once I make a decision, I often question if I made the right decision.

_____ When making a decision, I consider how it will affect others before me.

_____ I am often fearful that I may disappoint others.

_____ I find it challenging to say "NO" --I have not accepted that it is a complete sentence with no explanation needed.

_____ When it comes to speaking up for myself, I keep my feelings to myself.

_____ I struggle with delegating to others instead I handle everything myself.

_____ I find it challenging to put "ME" first.

_____ When the day ends and I have not completed my "to do" list I feel defeated.

_____ I don't often take risks because, I am afraid of failing.

_____ **Total your points:**

Remember this is an opportunity for you to discover where you are now and where you desire to be.

Inner-Confidence Assessment Key

Scoring:

50-41   You are confident in who you are. Continue showing up in your power. Keep soaring in your greatness!

40-31   You are discovering your Inner-Confidence! Focus on the areas you had low scores and begin taking action steps to grow. Support in these areas could prepare you for the next level.

30-21   Your confidence is developing. However, you often put others' needs ahead of your own and often get stuck in your mind. Coaching can help you develop the skills, tools, and strategies to Unlocking Your Inner-Confidence.

20-below You are caring and have a big heart, but your self-doubt, fear, and beliefs often leaves you questioning whether your ideas are worthy. Today I declare that your thoughts and ideas have true value. Coaching can help you develop and unlock your inner-confidence – as you prepare to walk in your greatness.

Inner-Confidence Checklist

☐ Eliminate Negative Self-Talk – Take control of your mind today by speaking positive thoughts whenever you begin to hear negative thoughts.

☐ Eliminate Valuing your Success in Comparison to Others – Remember everyone else is already taken so be the best you.

☐ Eliminate Self-Doubt – The world is waiting for you to stop doubting yourself and discover your greatness.

☐ Eliminate Focusing on your Weaknesses – Don't focus on your weaknesses, but instead embrace the greatness you have discovered as a result of them.

☐ Eliminate the Walls Blocking Your Passion – When you realize your passion is in fact the doorway to God's purpose for your life.

☐ Eliminate the Need to Be Perfect – Recognize that mistakes teach you lessons, disappointments make you wiser, and detours often lead you to your destination.

☐ Eliminate the Need to Hide Your Story – Share your story from a place of service, so that others may be served. Remember that while it is your story, it does not belong to you.

☐ Eliminate the Fear of Taking Bigger Risks – Life is about you taking risk to pursue your dreams, goals, and passions; you have nothing to lose but disappointment if you don't try.

☐ Eliminate the Fear of Failing – Remember it is ok to fail; in fact, that is where you will discover more about you.

☐ Eliminate the Need for Acceptance – Stop waiting on others to validate your worth and acknowledge the gifts God has given you.

Declare and Decree...

Today I Walk In My Confidence...
as I Embrace all God has in store for me

Today I Walk In My Confidence...
as I Show Up In My Power

Today I Walk In My Confidence...
as I Walk In My Greatness

Today I Walk In My Confidence...
as I stand bold, tall, & confident
as the Authentic Me

Today I Walk In My Confidence...
as I continue making a difference

Today I Walk In My Confidence...
as I grow, overcome, and most importantly serve

Today I Walk In My Confidence...
as I celebrate my past and the lessons I learned
along the way that has allowed me to make it to
this day of fulfillment

Today I Walk In My Confidence...
as I celebrate every step I have taken
in my journey

Declare and Decree...

Today I Walk In My Confidence...
as I allow my Faith to Shine brighter
than my Fear

Today I Walk In My Confidence...
as I allow my Faith to continue me on a journey
of purpose filled with expectation and excitement
of what God has in store for me

Today I Walk In My Confidence...
as I drown out all the voices and listen for the
one voice that matters – God's

Today I Walk In My Confidence...
as I seek Your wisdom and guidance on what
direction You will have me to serve

Today I Walk In My Confidence...
as I listen for Your word and direction
help me to stand still and embrace the wins
You have in store for me

Today I Walk In My Confidence...
as I stand on Your promise that no weapon
formed against me shall prosper

Declare and Decree...

Today I Walk In My Confidence...
as I draw closer to you God, I pray that You will
continue to wrap me in Your loving arms

Today I Walk In My Confidence...
as I move forward in my next level, God help me
find my way

Today I Walk In My Confidence...
as I celebrate all You have done, are doing, and
planning to do in my life

Today I Walk In My Confidence...
as I embrace the fact that I deserve all You have in
store for me

Today I Walk In My Confidence...
as I celebrate that You saw fit Lord God to use
even ME despite my scars and bruises

Today I Walk In My Confidence...
as I acknowledge that I have made some mistakes
but when the lights dimmed You reminded me to
turn on my high beams and shine brightly

Congratulations on your willingness to

"Unlock Your Inner-Confidence"

Are you READY to soar in your greatness UNAPOLOGETI-CALLY now that you have unlocked your keys? Today is your day to walk CONFIDENTLY in your GREATNESS. I am looking forward to going on a journey of empowerment together as confident women who are ready to show up authentically in our power without apology as we FEARLESSLY STRUT with POWER, POISE, & PURPOSE!

I look forward to staying connected with you! You can find me on all social media platforms FEARLESSLY STRUTTING IN CONFIDENCE WITH POWER, POISE, & PURPOSE:

Twitter, Instagram, & Persicope: @ReginaRSpeaks
Facebook: ReginaRobinsonSpeaks
Email: info@reginarobinsonspeaks.com
Website: www.reginarobinsonspeaks.com

FEARLESSY STRUTTING WITH
POWER, POISE, & PURPOSE!!

Only as high as you reach can you grow,
Only as far as you seek can you go,
Only as deep as you look can you see,
Only as much as you dream can you be.

—KAREN RAVN

60830876R00070

Made in the USA
Charleston, SC
05 September 2016